We Work at the
Fire Station

Angela Aylmore

Heinemann
LIBRARY

Little Nippers

H **www.heinemann.co.uk/library**
Visit our website to find out more information about **Heinemann Library** books.

To order:
☎ Phone 44 (0) 1865 888066
▤ Send a fax to 44 (0) 1865 314091
▥ Visit the Heinemann Bookshop at www.heinemann.co.uk/library to browse our catalogue and order online.

First published in Great Britain by Heinemann Library, Halley Court, Jordan Hill, Oxford OX2 8EJ, part of Harcourt Education.
Heinemann is a registered trademark of Harcourt

Editorial: Isabel Thomas and Sarah Chappelow
Design: Jo Hinton-Malivoire and bigtop
Picture Research: Erica Newbery
Production: Duncan Gilbert

Originated by RMW
Printed and bound in China by South China Printing Company

10 digit ISBN: 0 431 16488 6
13 digit ISBN: 978 0 431 16488 5
10 09 08 07 06
10 9 8 7 6 5 4 3 2 1

British Library Cataloguing in Publication Data
Aylmore, Angela
We work at the fire station. - (Where we work)
628.9'2
A full catalogue record for this book is available from the British Library.

Acknowledgements
The publishers would like to thank the following for permission to reproduce photographs:
Alamy pp. **6–7** (Ace Stock Limited), **20** (Blue Shadows); Corbis pp. **4–5** (George Hall), **8** (Robert Maass) **11**, **12–13** (Joseph Sohm/ ChromoSohm Inc.), **14–15** (Ted Horowitz); Getty Images pp. **17** (Photodisc), **20** top (Photodisc); Photoedit p. **21** top (Bill Aron); Shout pp. **18–19**.

Quiz pp. **22–23**: **astronaut** (Getty/Photodisc), **brush and comb** (Corbis/DK Limited), **doctor** (Getty Images/Photodisc), **firefighter helmet** (Corbis), **ladder** (Corbis/Royalty Free), **scrubs** (Corbis), **space food** (Alamy/Hugh Threlfall), **stethoscope** (Getty Images/Photodisc), **thermometer** (Getty Images/Photodisc).

Cover photograph of a firefighter reproduced with permission of Corbis/Ted Horowitz.

Every effort has been made to contact copyright holders of any material reproduced in this book. Any omissions will be rectified in subsequent printings if notice is given to the publishers.

The paper used to print this book comes from sustainable resources.

Some words are shown in bold, **like this**. They are explained in the glossary on page 24.

Contents

Welcome to the fire station!

This is a fire station.

4

Who do you think works here?

Working in the fire station

We are fire fighters. We work in the fire station.

The alarm

The **alarm** rings
when there is a fire.

RING!!!

ZOOOOM!

The pole helps us to get
downstairs quickly.

Getting dressed

We have to wear special clothes.

They keep us safe from smoke and flames.

helmet

mask

jacket

gloves

boots

11

All aboard the engine!

This is the fire engine.

ladders

hose reel

lights

siren

engine

The lights and **siren** tell people we are in a hurry.

Using the hose

We use water to
put out most fires.

We spray the water from a **hose**.

15

The ladders

Some buildings are very tall.

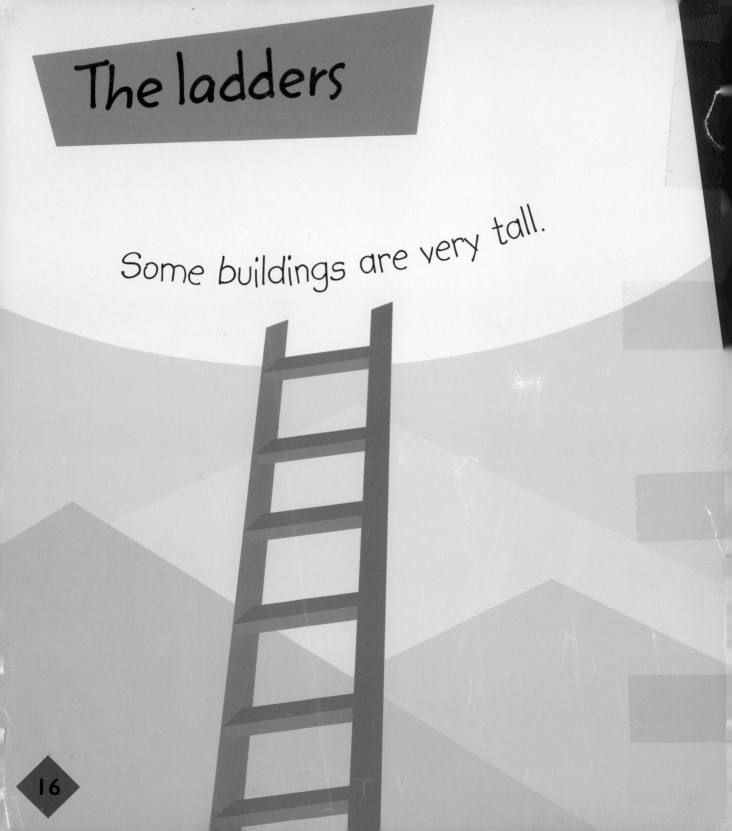

We use ladders
to help us
rescue people.

Back at the station

When the fire is out, we go back to the station.

We must get ready for the next **emergency**.

We have to wash the fire engine.

Stay safe

Never play with **matches** or anything hot.
You might start a fire.

Do not go near a
fire if you see one.
Who should you call?

Quiz

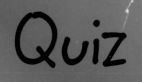

space food

Do you want to be a fire fighter? Which of these things would you need?

stethoscope

spacesuit

helmet

ladder

combs and
brushes

nurse's uniform

white coat

thermometer

23

Glossary

alarm loud bell that rings

emergency something serious and sudden

hose long, bendy pipe that carries water

matches short stick of wood for making fire

rescue save

siren loud noise a fire engine makes

Index

Notes for adults

This series supports the young child's exploration of their learning environment and their knowledge and understanding of their world. The following Early Learning Goals are relevant to the series:

• Respond to significant experiences, showing a range of feelings where appropriate.
• Find out about events they observe.
• Ask questions about why things happen and how things work.
• Find out and identify the uses of everyday technology to support their learning.

The series shows the different jobs professionals do in four different environments. There are opportunities to compare and contrast the jobs and provide an understanding of what each entails.

The books will help the child to extend their vocabulary, as they will hear new words. Some of the words that may be new to them in **We Work at the Fire Station** are *emergency, alarm, siren, hose, flames, rescue,* and *smoke.* Since the words are used in context in the book this should enable the young child to gradually incorporate them into their own vocabulary.

Follow-up activities

The child could role play situations at a fire station. They could imagine the different emergencies a fire fighter might encounter, such as putting out a fire or rescuing an animal. The child could also record what they have found out by drawing, painting, or tape recording their experiences.

24

Titles in the *Where We Work* series include:

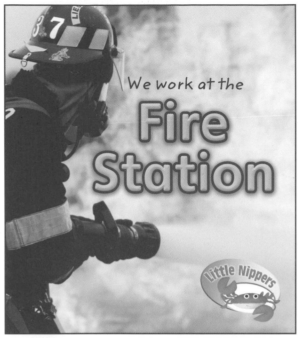

Hardback: 0-431-16488-6

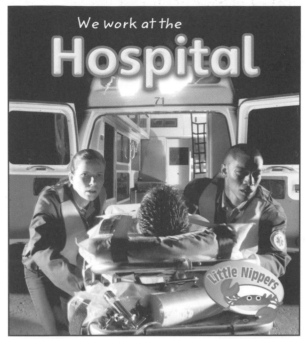

Hardback: 0-431-16489-4

Hardback: 0-431-16490-8

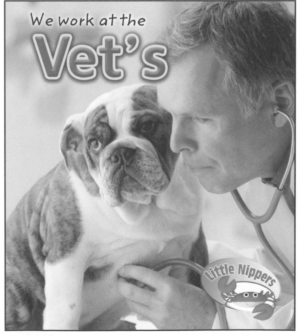

Hardback: 0-431-16491-6

Find out about other titles from Heinemann Library on our website www.heinemann.co.uk/library